A Macdonald book

First published 1976
Reprinted 1977, 1979,
    1982, 1983, 1985
Macdonald & Co
    (Publishers) Ltd
Maxwell House
Worship Street
London EC2A 2EN
A BPCC plc company

© Macdonald Educational
Limited, 1976

ISBN 0 356 05109 9
    (cased edition)
ISBN 0 356 06504 9
    (limp edition)

Made and printed by
New Interlitho s.p.a.
Milan
Italy

Editors
Verity Weston
Kate Woodhouse

Design
Ruth Prentice

Editorial Assistant
Julia Kirk

Production
Rosemary Bishop

Illustrators
Dick Eastland/Faulkner Marks
Ron Hayward Associates
Richard Hook/Faulkner Marks
Peter North
Tony Payne
Peter Thornley

Consultant
Harry Strongman,
Senior Lecturer in History
Berkshire College of
Education

Photographs
Scandinavian Airlines: 10, 30 (B), 37
J. Allan Cash: 12, 46(T)
Photoresources: 16, 27, 46(B)
ATA: 26, 31
Norwegian Maritime Museum: 30(T)

National Museum of Antiquities, Scotland: 40
University Collection of National Antiquities, Oslo: 45
National Museum, Copenhagen: 50
Icelandic Photo Service: 54
Photo Ellebe: 55
Ashmolean Museum: 23

The Vikings

Michael Gibson

Macdonald Educational

The Vikings

The Viking Age lasted from AD 790 to 1100. At the beginning of this period, Scandinavia was ruled by many petty kings. As the years went by, the states of Norway, Sweden and Denmark emerged. By the 840s, Vikings from Norway and Denmark were assembling large fleets and attacking many of the richest cities in Europe. These were ruthlessly plundered and then usually burnt to the ground.

At the same time, some Vikings, particularly Norwegians, were settling in the Scottish Isles. From Norway, they made their way to Iceland, Greenland and finally America. This was a magnificent achievement for a people without compasses or charts.

In the 860s, Swedish Vikings established themselves in Russia and began a flourishing trade with Arab and Byzantine merchants. Soon, Viking fleets were terrorizing the Black Sea and Caspian Sea as well as the Mediterranean and North Sea.

Although raiding continued, many Vikings settled down in the lands they visited. Vikings went to live in the British Isles, France, Iceland, Greenland and Russia. This book describes how the Vikings lived during the years of their greatness. The Vikings did not leave as much visible evidence as the Greeks and Romans, but archaeologists are finding objects which are adding to our knowledge almost daily. In addition, there are many superb Scandinavian poems and sagas.

The text and illustrations in this book are all based on these sources. Together, they give us a picture of what it was like to be a Viking during the Viking Age. They also explain why the people who lived in the lands which the Vikings raided were so frightened of the fierce warriors.

Contents

Terror from the sea

In 793, unexpectedly, a Viking raiding party landed on the small island of Lindisfarne, off north-east England. They attacked the monastery there and, to the horror of the monks, plundered the church of its treasures. They killed some of the monks and led others off to a life of slavery. Even worse, according to the Anglo-Saxon historian, Symeon of Durham, "they trampled upon the holy places with their filthy feet and dug up the altars". This raid was a warning of worse to come.

At the time of the Lindisfarne raid, much of Europe was ruled by Charlemagne, the king of the Franks. As long as Charlemagne lived, the Vikings did not dare make anything more than sudden smash-and-grab raids on his lands. As soon as Charlemagne died in 814 his sons started to quarrel over his empire. They were so busy fighting each other that they were quite unprepared to defend themselves against the Viking attacks. The Vikings were able to sail up the great rivers of Europe and raid and pillage the peaceful countryside. These raids greatly increased the power of the Vikings. For the next two hundred years the Vikings raided, fought and lived throughout Europe.

▼ The Vikings pulled their longships up on to the beach and rushed forward to attack the monastery. The monks were caught by surprise for, as an Anglo-Saxon pointed out at the time: "It is some 350 years that we and our forefathers have lived in this lovely land and never before has such a terror appeared in Britain."

Homelands of the Vikings

The people we call the Vikings lived in Scandinavia, that is, present-day Norway, Sweden and Denmark. Although the three countries were linked together in many ways, each country was independent of the others.

No one is certain of the meaning of the word *Viking*. It may come from the Old Icelandic word *vik* which means *bay* or *creek*. A Viking was therefore someone who lurked with his ship in a bay. Some people think it comes from the Anglo-Saxon word *wic*, meaning camp, so that a Viking would mean an armed warrior.

However, the Scandinavians did not call themselves Vikings. This name was given to them by early writers. They would probably have taken their name from the area in which they lived.

▲ To seal a bargain, Vikings slapped hands. This still happe[n] in France, Denmark and Englar[d]

◄ The long, narrow inlets along the coasts of Norway, Iceland and Greenland are called fiords. They are usually very deep but become shallower towards their mouths. They were probably formed by glaciers millions of years ago.

▶ Little land in Scandinavia is suitable for farming. Norway is very mountainous, Sweden is densely forested and Denmark has large areas of infertile heathland. Settlements were usually nea[r] the coast, some were further north than the Arctic Circle.

▲ One of the possible reasons for the Vikings' expansion abroad was the shortage of farming land at home.

▲ The skill the Vikings developed in building boats enabled them to travel long distances overseas to distant lands.

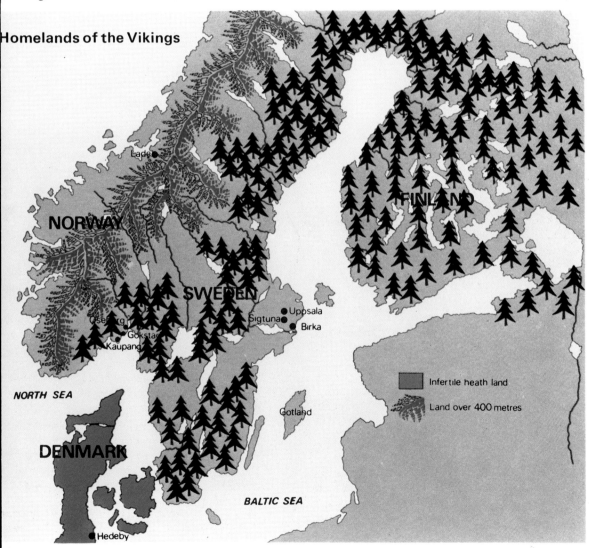

Homelands of the Vikings

NORWAY

SWEDEN

FINLAND

DENMARK

NORTH SEA

BALTIC SEA

Lade

Oseberg
Gokstad
Kaupang

Sigtuna
Uppsala
Birka

Gotland

Hedeby

Infertile heath land

Land over 400 metres

The rules of society

Viking ranks

▲ At the beginning of the Viking age, petty kings ruled most of Scandinavia.

▲ Karls were rich freemen and farmers. They ranked midway between kings and jarls.

▲ Jarls were the most important group of people. They owned their own land.

▲ Thralls were slaves. Their owners had the power of life and death over them.

The family was the most important group within Viking society. People would make decisions for the good of their family, not just for their own good. As the Vikings were very proud people, there were frequent quarrels between families. At the *thing* or local assembly, a feud might be settled after both families had put forward their case. The *thing* decided who was to blame by listening to the witnesses.

Sometimes people were required to undergo ordeal to prove that they were telling the truth. Women were sometimes asked to pick stones out of vats of boiling water. Their hands were bandaged for a time and then examined in public. If the wound was clean, they had been telling the truth. People who were found guilty were punished according to the law. Most criminals were fined or banished from the country. The fines were fixed to cover every possible injury.

▲ This is the site of the Icelandic *Althing* or National Assembly. It first met in 930 at the north end of Lake Olfusvatn. It was a law court and a parliament.

▲ If a man were killed, his family felt that it was their duty to avenge his death. Such a feud might go on for many years.

▲ Sometimes quarrels were settled by duels. The duellists struck each other in turn until one gave in or was killed.

▲ Some feuds were ended by the guilty party paying fines for the wrong done. The money had to be paid in public.

▲ *Things* were assemblies of freemen where matters of importance were discussed. They were both law courts and local councils.

Table of fines

All Viking goods were valued at a certain amount, like these dogs. Anyone caught stealing had to pay back the value of what he had taken.

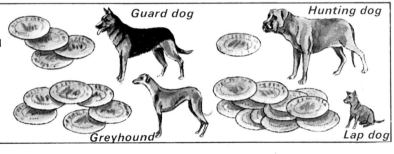

Guard dog

Hunting dog

Greyhound

Lap dog

Living on the farmstead

Viking farms were usually small, with a number of fields and vegetable patches. Much of the soil was very poor so the land needed a great deal of care. The farmers grew barley and oats, and in some areas, rye. In summer they cut the corn with sickles and scythes. The ears of corn were separated from the stalks and stored until needed. They were ground into flour by hand-querns. The farmers also grew peas and cabbages on their vegetable patches, and apple, hazel and walnut trees. The nuts and fruit could be stored for use in the winter.

Cattle were just as important to the farmer as corn. In addition to meat, they provided milk which could be made into butter and cheese. The long, cold winters and poor soil in Scandinavia meant that farming was very hard work.

▼ The central point of this farmstead on a Norwegian fiord is the long house. The smaller houses are used as workshops or shelters for the animals. In summer the families tending the cattle in the mountains lived in rough stone or wood shelters.

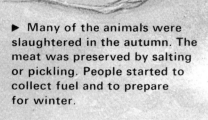

▲ When spring came the Vikings started to sow their crops. First they broke up the soil with hand ploughs or with ploughs drawn by oxen, then they sowed the seed by hand.

▶ Many of the animals were slaughtered in the autumn. The meat was preserved by salting or pickling. People started to collect fuel and to prepare for winter.

► Much of the summer was spent preparing for the winter. The families drove their cattle up to the rich mountain pastures to graze. They made the milk into butter and cheese for the winter.

► In winter, the Vikings went hunting on their skis. Some, like this man, made tools and weapons out of wood and iron.

Store house

Long house

Byre

Forge

able garden

Wood pile

Bath house

Home field

Houses of turf and timber

Most Vikings lived in rectangular houses with walls made either of turves, upright timbers, wattle and daub or stone. Their roofs were formed of rafters covered with thatch, wooden shingles or turves.

In the early days these houses only had one room. The head of the family slept in a box bed, but everyone else slept on raised platforms running round the sides of the room. They cooked in a fire pit in the middle of the floor. The smoke from the fire escaped through a small hole in the roof. A little light came in through tiny slits in the walls. These were hung with weapons and sometimes with cloth hangings, showing the adventures of famous warriors. The floor was covered with reeds and herbs.

The houses had hardly any furniture. In the middle of one wall there was a place where only the head of the family could sit on his own special chair. Everyone else sat on simple benches or on the fur-covered raised platforms which were often built along the sides.

Later, the houses were divided into separate rooms. Although this made the houses more comfortable, they still remained dark, smelly and smoky.

Types of houses

▼ The Vikings built many different kinds of houses. The design of the houses depended on the climate and the kinds of materials that were available. Where trees were plentiful, the houses were usually built of wood. The houses shown below are three types of Viking house.

▲ Curved-wall long houses were made of split tree trunks set in upright rows. The roof was supported by the walls and additional posts set at an angle to the wall.

▲ Stave houses had walls made of vertical staves or planks.

▲ Some houses had walls built of horizontal planks laid between vertical wooden posts.

▲ This turf-covered house in Iceland shows how many of the Vikings' houses must have looked.

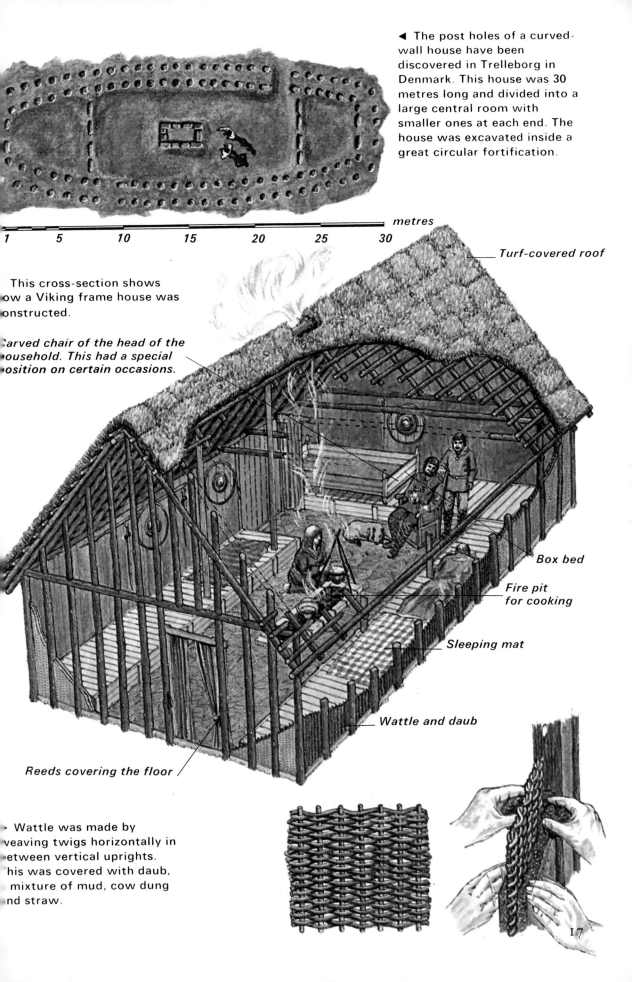

◄ The post holes of a curved-wall house have been discovered in Trelleborg in Denmark. This house was 30 metres long and divided into a large central room with smaller ones at each end. The house was excavated inside a great circular fortification.

metres

1   5   10   15   20   25   30

This cross-section shows how a Viking frame house was constructed.

Carved chair of the head of the household. This had a special position on certain occasions.

Turf-covered roof

Box bed

Fire pit for cooking

Sleeping mat

Wattle and daub

Reeds covering the floor

► Wattle was made by weaving twigs horizontally in between vertical uprights. This was covered with daub, a mixture of mud, cow dung and straw.

Family life

Viking families ate, slept, cooked and worked in the one room of their house. The two most important objects in the room would have been the fire pit for cooking and the loom for weaving. There were no cupboards in the room. Belongings were either hung on the walls or stored in chests around the edge of the room.

Most of the cooking was done inside the house, though bread was sometimes baked in an oven outside. A typical Viking meal might have been thick slices of bread and butter, roast or boiled meat of wild boar, red deer, elk or even bear, with vegetables or fruit. They drank skim milk or buttermilk and whey, as well as beer and a strong drink made from honey called mead. The Vikings enjoyed sweet food and as they had no sugar they used honey in their cooking.

After cooking, weaving was the most important activity in the house. The women spun the wool and wove it into cloth. Then they made the cloth into clothes, wall hangings or coverings for the benches around the walls.

▶ The interior of a Viking house

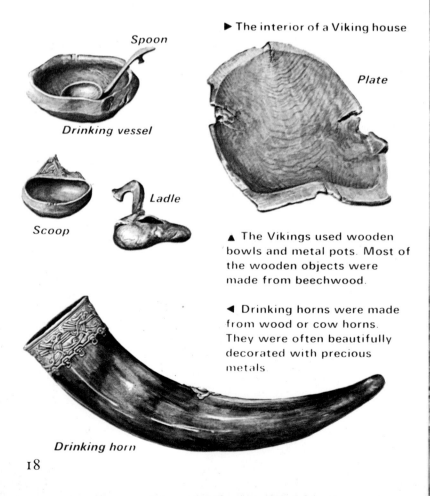

Spoon

Drinking vessel

Scoop

Ladle

Plate

▲ The Vikings used wooden bowls and metal pots. Most of the wooden objects were made from beechwood.

◀ Drinking horns were made from wood or cow horns. They were often beautifully decorated with precious metals.

Drinking horn

Clothes and jewellery

The Vikings were proud of their appearance and liked to dress well. Most of their clothes were made of wool or linen that they had spun and woven themselves. The cloth was dyed with mineral or vegetable dyes of green, brown, red, yellow or blue.

The men wore sleeved jerkins or three-quarter length coats over woollen shirts and long cloth trousers. On their feet they wore tall leather boots or soft shoes with short socks. The women wore long woollen dresses and linen tunics which reached down to their ankles. Their legs and feet were covered with thick woolly socks and soft leather shoes. Both men and women wore fur or woollen hats and cloaks when they went out in cold weather. Cloaks were fastened at the shoulder with brooches. Children probably wore the same kind of clothes as their parents.

Everyone liked to wear gold and silver brooches, bracelets, necklaces, armbands and rings. Some of their jewellery was part of the loot from raids on foreign churches and monasteries.

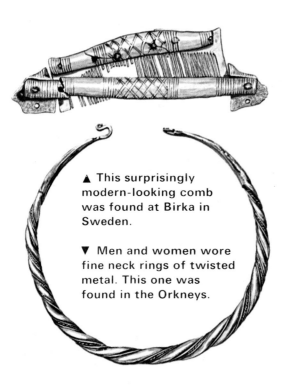

▲ This surprisingly modern-looking comb was found at Birka in Sweden.

▼ Men and women wore fine neck rings of twisted metal. This one was found in the Orkneys.

▼ These people probably belong to a fairly rich family. Poor people would have worn similar clothes, but their jewellery and the embroidery on their tunics would probably have been less ornate.

▲ This bronze brooch has been decorated with sheet silver. It was probably worn by a rich woman, between two oval brooches.

▲ This gold filigree brooch was found at Hornelund in Denmark. Women wore such brooches on each shoulder.

▲ This thistle brooch is a good example of Viking jewellery. It is made from silver and was found in Ireland.

Children growing up

In Viking society, people usually lived in large famil[y] groups. This consisted of three generations; childre[n] parents and grandparents. The head of the househo[ld] was responsible for the wellbeing of the family. He ha[d] to look after and provide for his wife, children an[d] parents. Sometimes he was expected to help his brother[s] and sisters as well.

His wife had to look after the younger children, pr[e]pare and cook the food, clean the house and wash th[e] clothes. She also milked the cows, and made the butt[er] and cheese. She was expected to make medicines an[d] care for the sick and wounded. When her husband w[as] away she was in charge of the household and wore th[e] keys at her waist as a sign of her authority.

▼ Viking children did not go to school, but that does not mean that they had an easy life. As soon as they were able they were expected to help their parents. The boys helped with the farm and the girls with the work inside the house.

▲ Naming a baby was important. The name was supposed to decide a baby's character.

▲ Girls were taught to spin and weave so they could help to make the family's clothe[s]

▲ Boys had to learn to plough a straight furrow and to cut wood with an adze.

▲ Children learned about their ancestors from the stories the old people told them.

The way in which the children were treated depended very much upon their father. He had complete control over them. Some children were treated harshly and others leniently. Viking boys were expected to be "manly". This seems to have meant having a mind of their own and standing up for what they believed in. Girls, on the other hand, were expected to be quiet and obedient. Fathers usually chose husbands for their daughters, although girls were rarely forced to marry men they did not like, and could choose to divorce their husband if they wished.

When things went wrong, the local people usually helped out. In Iceland, if a man lost all his cattle through disease, his neighbours gave him some of theirs. If a man lost his money, his relations were expected to help him back on his feet again. During hard times it was the parents and children who came first. Occasionally old people and newly-born babies were left to die, since the available food was needed for the young and healthy people.

▲ This game board is probably Scandinavian, but the counters were brought from Egypt.

Carving the runes

◄ The Runic alphabet or *futhark* was invented about 2,000 years ago. Originally there were 24 letters, but by about AD 900 only 16 letters were used. Runes were carved on memorial stones. Some of these stones have been found in Sweden and Norway. The runes on this stone say: "Torsten caused this monument to be made in memory of Sven his father and of Tove his brother who went out of Greece and of Ingetora his mother. Ybber engraved it."

▲ Runes were cut into pieces of wood or stone with a knife or chisel.

▼ The Runic alphabet

ᚠ ᚢ ᚦ ᚨ ᚱ ᚴ ᚼ ᚾ ᛁ ᛅ ᛋ ᛏ ᛒ ᛘ ᛚ ᛦ

f u th q r k h n i a s t b m l R

Hedeby: the great market

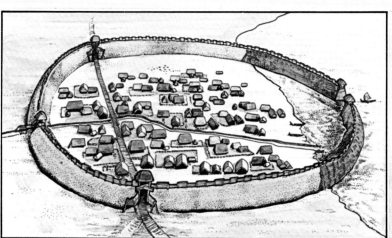

◀ Hedeby was surrounded by a wall of earth. This was so high and thick that people ha to walk through tunnels in it. There was also a strong sea wall made of wood. This protected the town from attack and provided shelter for ships.

Not every Viking lived in a tiny farmstead or village. Many lived in large towns like Kaupang in Norway, Birka in Sweden and Hedeby in Denmark. Hedeby was one of the most important towns in the Viking world. It was built at the foot of the Jutland peninsula facing the Baltic Sea.

The people of Hedeby were merchants and craftsmen. Some craftsmen made brooches, pendants and little figures, others were expert glassblowers, horn carvers and clothmakers. Viking merchants brought goods from Germany, France, Norway, England, Constantinople and Persia to trade at Hedeby. Arabs came from Spain and the Middle East to buy slaves, as Hedeby was the chief centre for the slave trade. People would visit Hedeby from all over Scandinavia to buy jewellery, fine cloth and other goods.

▼ **Hedeby was built by the side of the Schlei Fiord. We** have a fairly good idea of what it probably looked like from the remains that have been dug up there. There were at least two main streets paved with logs, with both large and small houses. Most of the houses had several storage huts or work places with their own well. These were all enclosed by a wooden fence

The Viking craftsman

Each farmer was probably his own smith and carpenter, but there were also highly skilled men who specialized in these crafts. Carpenters were very important as boat and house builders, smiths for making weapons and jewellery. The Viking raids depended on the skills of these men for their boats and weapons.

Wood was one of the most popular materials in Scandinavia because it was so readily available. Once the trees were felled, they were split into sections with wedges. The wood was then shaped with a tool called an adze. During the Viking age the Scandinavians produced magnificent wood carvings, both on their ships and on other objects.

To make a sword or an axe, the smith would heat a bar of iron until it was white hot, hammer it and plunge it into cold water to cool it quickly. He repeated this process until the weapon was hard. Fine weapons were greatly prized and handed down from father to son.

▲ This axe is decorated in the Mammen style of 960 to 1020

▼ This carpenter's tool set was found in Sweden. The tools have changed so little that craftsmen today would find them easy to use.

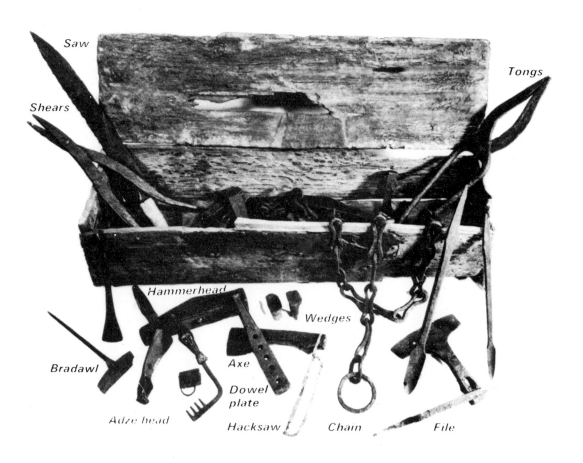

Decorating an axe

The Vikings often decorated their weapons with bronze, brass or silver. To do this, the weapon was first heated over a fire until it was black

▲ The design was cut into the surface with a sharp instrument. Small pieces of silver, bronze or brass were rubbed into the hot grooves until they stuck.

▲ The weapon was put back into the fire, and polished with a long tool of smooth steel. This was repeated until the decoration shone.

▲ These scenes were carved in wood on the doorway of Hylestad church in Norway. They show Sigurd, a Viking hero, testing his sword on an anvil. The sword breaks and Regin, the smith, has to forge another blade. Sigurd uses the new sword to kill a dragon guarding some treasure.

In search of treasure

Uppsala
Birka

Kaupang

No

Hedeby

Cracow

Prague

Mainz

Noirmoutier

▲ Rich Vikings drank out of glasses like this one, brought from Germany.

One of the most important routes developed by the Swedish Vikings was southwards through Russia. Each year the Vikings set out with ships laden with furs, wax, honey and slaves. They sailed up the rivers of northern Russia and carried their boats overland to the head of the River Dnieper. They followed the river to the Black Sea and sailed across to Constantinople, where they sold their goods and bought wines and brocades.

Other ships sailed down the River Volga to the Caspian Sea. Here they met Arab merchants from Baghdad, who sold them Persian glass, Chinese silks, Far Eastern spices and silver.

The Vikings travelled widely from all parts of Scandinavia, both on raids and in search of trade.

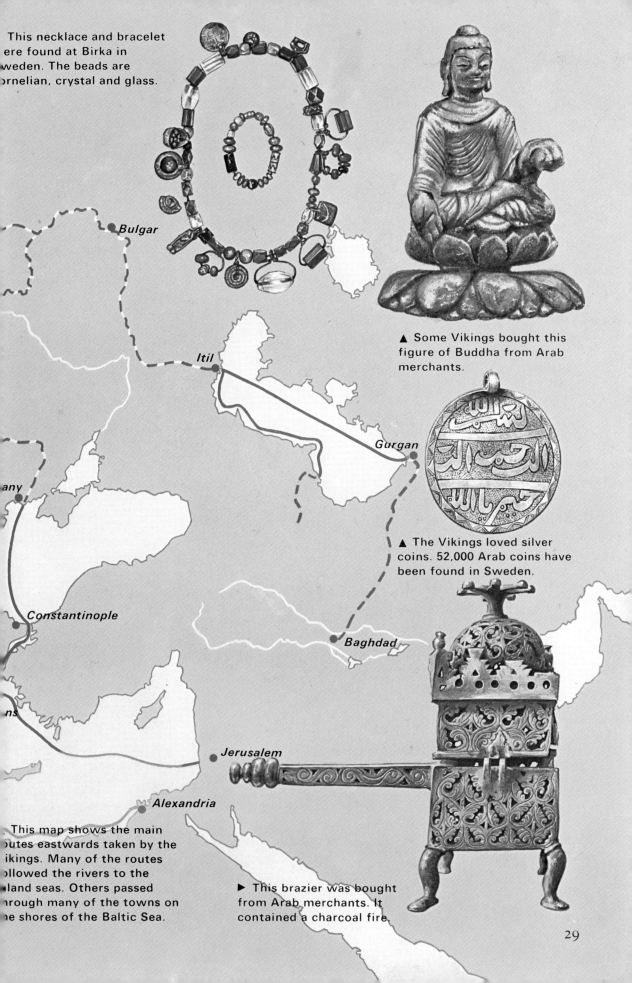

This necklace and bracelet
were found at Birka in
Sweden. The beads are
cornelian, crystal and glass.

Bulgar

Itil

Gurgan

Germany

Constantinople

Baghdad

Athens

Jerusalem

Alexandria

▲ Some Vikings bought this
figure of Buddha from Arab
merchants.

▲ The Vikings loved silver
coins. 52,000 Arab coins have
been found in Sweden.

This map shows the main
routes eastwards taken by the
Vikings. Many of the routes
followed the rivers to the
inland seas. Others passed
through many of the towns on
the shores of the Baltic Sea.

▶ This brazier was bought
from Arab merchants. It
contained a charcoal fire.

29

"Steeds of the waves"

Viking ships were among the finest ever built. There were several kinds for different uses. One of the best known is the longship, which was a canoe-like warship. It was long and thin and sat low in the water. Its prow and stern were carved in the shape of savage animals which were covered in gold and silver, and flashed in the sun. When the ship entered port, its sides were lined with gaily coloured shields. These were removed when the ship put out to sea. The longship had one large square sail, which was usually striped blue, red or green. Each ship had a set of oars and was rowed along in calm weather. The ship was steered by a large oar at the stern.

This reconstruction of the okstad ship was sailed across e Atlantic in 1893. The okstad ship was found in a urial mound in 1880. It was ot a specialized ship, and robably dates from the inth century.

The Gotland stone shows a iking ship with a chequered ail. The Vikings were probably ble to shorten or "reef" the ail by pulling on the ropes anging from the bottom of e sail.

The Oseberg ship was econstructed from excavated emains. The buried ship ontained the bodies of two omen and many of their ossessions, including beds, ankets and chests.

How the longship was built

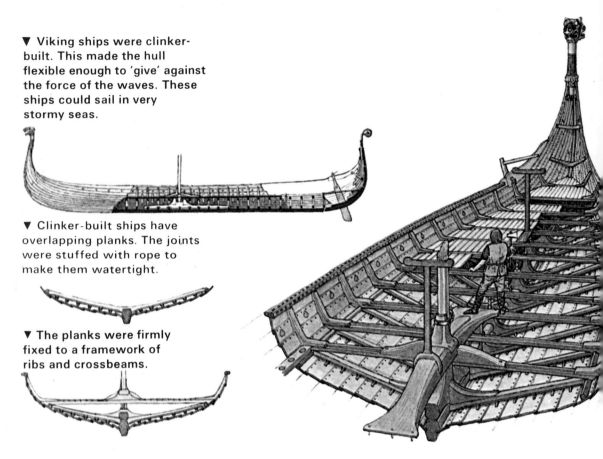

▼ Viking ships were clinker-built. This made the hull flexible enough to 'give' against the force of the waves. These ships could sail in very stormy seas.

▼ Clinker-built ships have overlapping planks. The joints were stuffed with rope to make them watertight.

▼ The planks were firmly fixed to a framework of ribs and crossbeams.

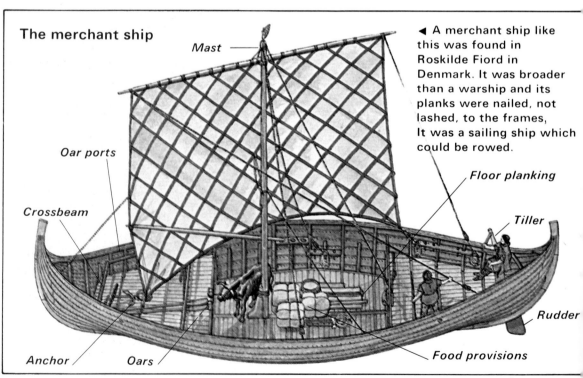

The merchant ship

◄ A merchant ship like this was found in Roskilde Fiord in Denmark. It was broader than a warship and its planks were nailed, not lashed, to the frames, It was a sailing ship which could be rowed.

Mast

Oar ports

Crossbeam

Anchor

Oars

Floor planking

Tiller

Rudder

Food provisions

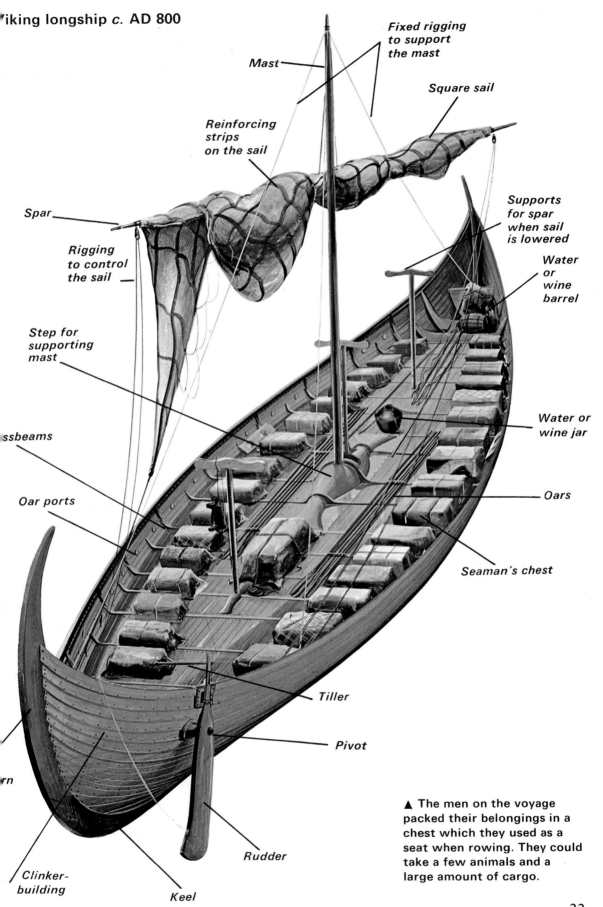

Viking longship c. AD 800

Mast

Fixed rigging
to support
the mast

Square sail

Reinforcing
strips
on the sail

Spar

Supports
for spar
when sail
is lowered

Rigging
to control
the sail

Water
or
wine
barrel

Step for
supporting
mast

Water or
wine jar

ssbeams

Oars

Oar ports

Seaman's chest

Tiller

Pivot

rn

Rudder

Clinker-
building

Keel

▲ The men on the voyage
packed their belongings in a
chest which they used as a
seat when rowing. They could
take a few animals and a
large amount of cargo.

Hunting sea mammals

The Vikings were expert hunters and fishermen. They hunted forest animals, marsh and coastland birds and fished for river and sea fish. Sea mammals, such as seals, walruses and whales, were the biggest game. Hunting and fishing went on, wherever possible, in winter and summer.

The people living in forest areas learned to recognize the "spoor" or footprints of the forest animals and their drinking and sleeping places. They tracked the animals down and killed them with their spears or bows and arrows. Around the marshes and coastland there were many wild ducks, geese and sea birds. These birds were probably netted and their eggs stolen from their nests.

The Vikings used baited lines, traps and nets to catch salmon and trout in the streams and lakes. They speared fish when the water was clear and shallow enough, and had fishing grounds in the fiords and offshore channels along the Norwegian coast and Baltic Sea.

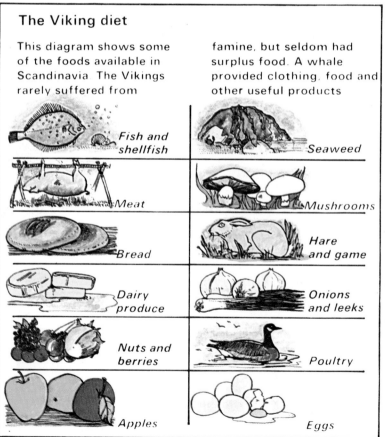

The Viking diet

This diagram shows some of the foods available in Scandinavia. The Vikings rarely suffered from famine, but seldom had surplus food. A whale provided clothing, food and other useful products

Fish and shellfish

Seaweed

Meat

Mushrooms

Bread

Hare and game

Dairy produce

Onions and leeks

Nuts and berries

Poultry

Apples

Eggs

▲ Seals and walruses could be caught in nets or speared, but whales were driven on to the shore.

New lands in the west

Viking exploration westwards

While some Vikings were raiding in Europe, others were exploring the Atlantic and discovering new lands. In about 860 a Swedish Viking called Gardar Svavarson was blown by a storm to the coast of Iceland. About fifteen years later, the first settlers started arriving. By 930 there were about 50,000 people living in Iceland.

In 982 Erik the Red sailed westwards from Iceland and discovered another larger island. He called it Greenland to make it sound attractive to settlers. Two colonies grew up in the area of the present-day town of Julianehab in the south and Godthab in the west. Eventually there were about 3,000 settlers in Greenland.

According to the sagas, Bjarni, an Icelander, caught sight of land to the west of Greenland. About fifteen years later Leif Erikson sailed west and discovered Helluland, Markland and Vinland. Historians think that these places are modern Baffin Island, Labrador and Newfoundland. For years historians did not know whether the Vinland sagas were based on fact. Then in 1962 a Viking settlement dating from about AD 1000 was discovered at L'Anse-aux-Meadows in Newfoundland. This seems to prove that the Vikings went to America.

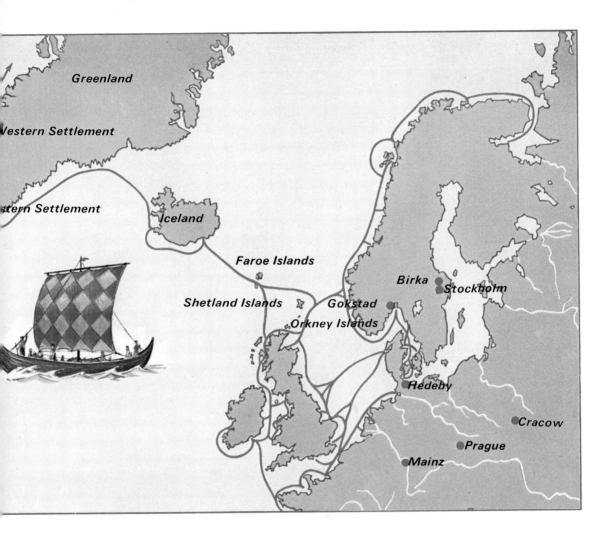

Greenland

Western Settlement

Eastern Settlement

Iceland

Faroe Islands

Shetland Islands

Orkney Islands

Gokstad

Birka

Stockholm

Hedeby

Cracow

Prague

Mainz

This map shows the routes the Vikings probably took westwards. We do not know the exact routes, but these are the most likely.

The Vinland sagas tell how the Indians offered fur and skins in exchange for red cloth and weapons. The Vikings would not sell their weapons. The Indians attacked the camp and drove the Vikings out.

The deadly icebergs in the North Atlantic were a great danger to the Viking ships.

Merciless raiders

Viking raids were famed and feared throughout Europe. The sight of a Viking ship sailing down a coast or up a river was dreaded by thousands of people. They knew that a Viking raid might mean that many of them would be killed defending themselves and that they would never see many of their prized possessions again.

The great age of the Viking raiders lasted from 790 to 880. After that time, many Vikings settled in the lands they attacked. Nevertheless, raiding continued until about AD 1100. By the 860s, the Vikings had permanent bases abroad, which meant they could stay away from Scandinavia for years at a time if necessary.

The raiders were usually farmers or full-time soldiers. Generally it was the Norwegians who raided the Scottish Islands, Scotland, Ireland, north-west England and the Mediterranean. The Danes attacked eastern England, Germany, the Netherlands and France, and the Swedes raided Russia and lands to the south.

▲ Hastein led a famous raid between 859 and 862. He left France with 62 ships.

▲ After a successful raid in France, they sailed for Italy. When they saw the magnificent city of Luna, they thought it was Rome. They attacked the city but were beaten back.

▲ Then Hastein pretended to be dying. He was baptized by one of the priests of Luna.

▲ He sailed south to Spain where he was defeated by the Arabs. He managed to enter the Mediterranean and plundered the coast of North Africa and Spain.

▲ The Vikings spent the winter on an island at the mouth of the river Rhone.

▲ Hastein's coffin was carried by Vikings into the town cemetery.

▲ Once in the town, Hastein leapt out of his coffin and his men drew their weapons.

They looted the city and Hastein returned to France laden with treasure.

The warrior and his weapons

The Vikings were fierce warriors with some of the best armour and weapons in Europe. They protected their bodies with tough leather tunics and occasionally with mail shirts. They wore simple conical helmets, not the winged helmets that are so often drawn by artists. They carried large round shields which were painted and sometimes covered with leather.

The most popular weapons were swords, spears and axes. Their long swords were sharpened along both edges. The spears were of two types: light throwing spears and heavy thrusting ones. The axes were fearsome weapons and could cut off an enemy's hands, feet or head. Bows and arrows were sometimes used to shoot enemies at long range.

The Vikings were among the most successful warriors in history, although they were badly defeated by the Arabs, Anglo-Saxons and Irish at various times.

▼ The Vikings built fine defensive fortifications. Fou such fortifications have beer excavated in Denmark. They all date from the late tenth or early eleventh centuries. They may have been used either as training bases or as places of refuge for soldiers.

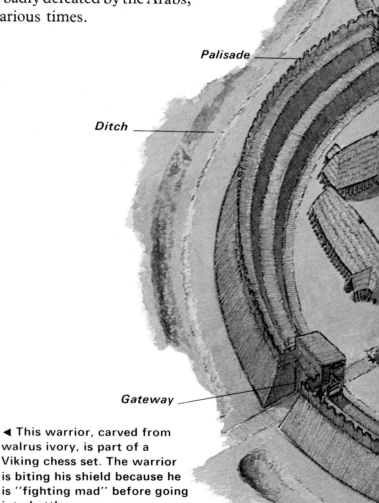

Palisade

Ditch

Gateway

◄ This warrior, carved from walrus ivory, is part of a Viking chess set. The warrior is biting his shield because he is "fighting mad" before going into battle.

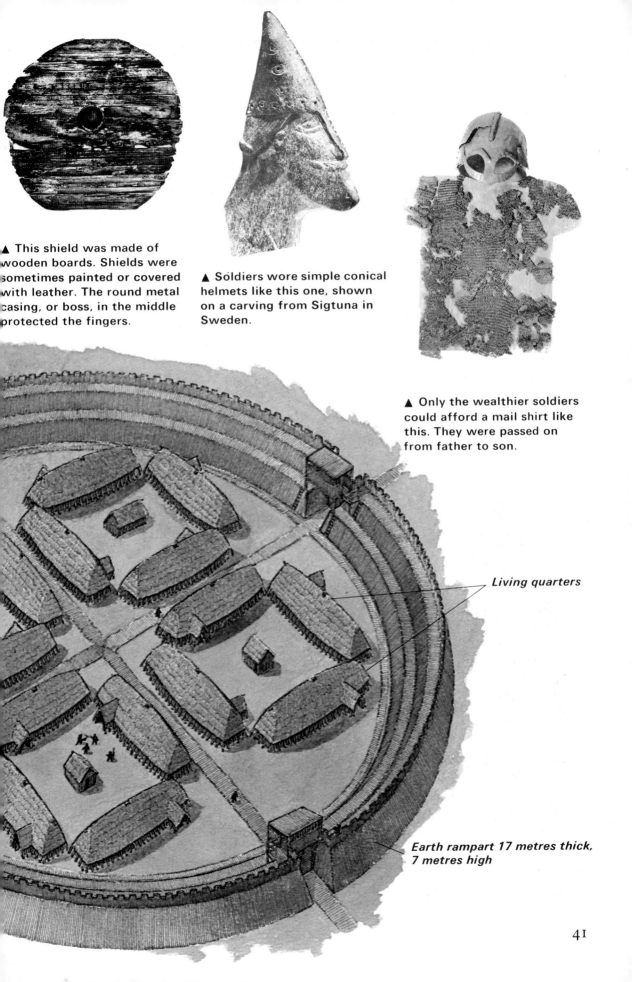

▲ This shield was made of wooden boards. Shields were sometimes painted or covered with leather. The round metal casing, or boss, in the middle protected the fingers.

▲ Soldiers wore simple conical helmets like this one, shown on a carving from Sigtuna in Sweden.

▲ Only the wealthier soldiers could afford a mail shirt like this. They were passed on from father to son.

Living quarters

Earth rampart 17 metres thick, 7 metres high

The role of women

Viking women were responsible for all the household duties: cooking, cleaning, washing and the care of young children. They also did the spinning and weaving of cloth and made clothes for the family. They probably learned these skills when they were children.

The women could be very independent, especially if they were from a wealthy family. They were allowed to own land and other valuables and to act as farmers and traders in their own right. In many countries at this time women were not allowed to do these things.

It was usually the women who taught their children stories, poetry and riddles. In this way they made sure that traditions were passed on to their children. Since very few people could read or write, this was the only way the Vikings had of passing on knowledge and stories.

► Sometimes the Vikings carved scenes from important people's lives on large stones. This imaginary picture stone tells the story of the life of Aud the Deep Minded, widow of King Olaf the White of Dublin. At the bottom, Aud is shown at the wedding of her grand-daughter, where there is feasting and rejoicing. Aud then sets sail for Iceland in her merchant ship. She buys land, and is shown in the top picture directing the ploughing and cultivation of her farmstead. When she dies, she is placed in a burial ship and covered with a huge mound of earth.

▲ When two people married, the man had to pay the bride's father a "bridesprice". This was a gift of cattle or gold.

▲ If a couple wanted to divorce they only had to tell witnesses that they wished to separate.

▲ The woman looked after the farmstead if the husband was away. She would defend the home against attack.

▲ Women traded with visiting merchants when their husbands were away on a raid, or if they were widows.

43

Death of a hero

When a Viking warrior died, he was buried with great splendour. His body was dressed in his best clothes and jewellery and laid in the grave. His weapons, tools and most precious possessions were placed beside him. The richer the Viking, the more magnificent his grave was. Wealthy people were buried in great wooden chambers with their favourite horse and dog and large amounts of food and drink. People think that these possessions were provided to help the man on his journey after death. Some Viking chieftains were buried in their ships. These ship burials provide a great deal of information about their lives and possessions.

▼ The Vikings believed that as soon as the body was burnt the spirit went to Valhalla. This was a heaven where warriors spent their time fighting and feasting. Warriors hoped to reach Valhalla by dying with a sword in their hand.

An Arab called Ibn Fadlan once watched a ship burial in Russia and wrote an account of what he saw. When he came to the place where the king was to be buried, he saw a fine ship drawn up on dry land and surrounded with firewood. The ship was filled with beautiful armour, weapons, carved chairs and beds. The body of the king was carried to the ship and laid on a fine couch. Then a number of horses, cows and dogs were sacrificed and their bodies thrown on to the ship. Lastly, a relative of the dead man stepped forward from the silent crowd and set light to the wood with a blazing torch. In a moment the ship and its contents blazed with flames and smoke until nothing but ashes remained. These were then covered with a mound of earth. Sometimes the ships were not burnt, just buried with their contents. Many of these burial ships have been discovered by archaeologists.

▲ This lion-headed post was one of four found on the Oseberg ship. It was probably to frighten off evil spirits.

◄ The Norwegian Oseberg ship was excavated in 1904. It was covered with a mound of peat, which preserved it.

The wagon from the Oseberg ship is the only one found. Its sides are carved with scenes from Norse myths.

45

Norse gods and legends

The Vikings believed that the world was ruled by gods who lived in a heavenly place called Asgard. The greatest of their gods was Odin. He was wise, cunning and dangerous and filled everyone with fear. He was only seen in battles or at other times of great danger. As he was the king of the gods, only those who believed they had supernatural power dared worship him.

Thor was a very different god. He carried a huge stone hammer called Mjollnir. Thor was the god of wind, rain and farming. When he rode across the sky in his enormous chariot drawn by goats, there was thunder and lightning. In spite of his tremendous strength and quick temper, Thor was a happy, rather stupid god. Thor's day, or Thursday in English, became the usual time for meetings and great feasts.

Frey was the god of marriage and growing things. When the Vikings sowed their crops they scattered bread and poured wine or beer on to the ground. They hoped this would please Frey so that he would make the crops grow tall and strong.

The Vikings had no churches or temples. They usually worshipped their gods outdoors where they believed there was no danger from evil spirits.

▲ This picture stone shows Odin racing across the sky on his eight-legged horse, Sleipnir. His wolves, Geri and Freki, went with him.

▶ There are many waterfalls in Scandinavia like Latefoss in Norway. The Vikings probably worshipped their gods beside waterfalls.

▲ The Valkyries were women sent by Odin to lead dead warriors to Valhalla, the Viking heaven.

▲ This bronze image of Frey, the god of fertility, was found in Sweden.

▲ This model of Thor's hammer would have been worn by a Viking as protection against evil spirits.

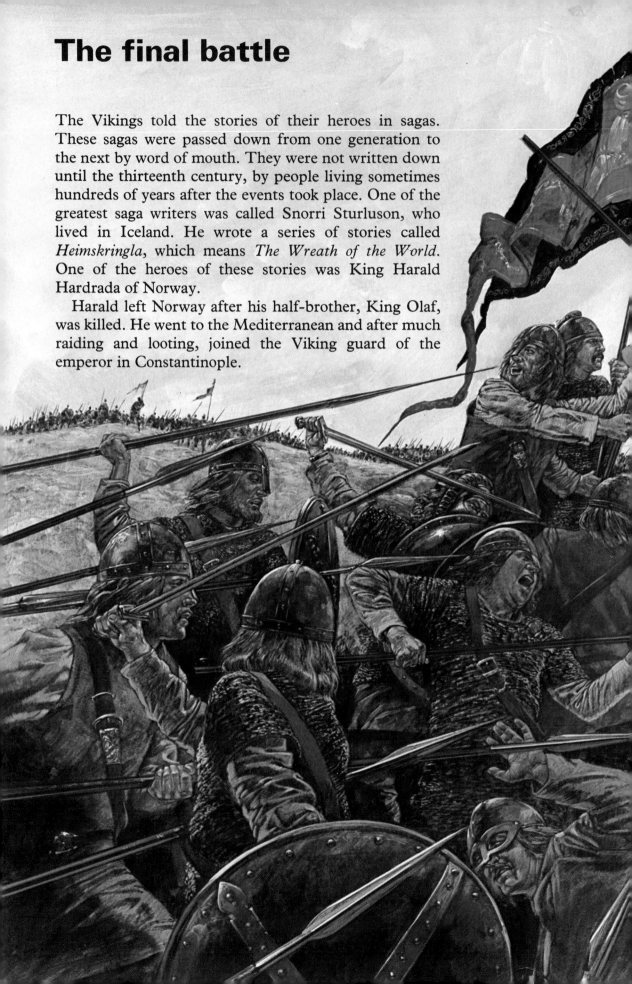

The final battle

The Vikings told the stories of their heroes in sagas. These sagas were passed down from one generation to the next by word of mouth. They were not written down until the thirteenth century, by people living sometimes hundreds of years after the events took place. One of the greatest saga writers was called Snorri Sturluson, who lived in Iceland. He wrote a series of stories called *Heimskringla*, which means *The Wreath of the World*. One of the heroes of these stories was King Harald Hardrada of Norway.

Harald left Norway after his half-brother, King Olaf, was killed. He went to the Mediterranean and after much raiding and looting, joined the Viking guard of the emperor in Constantinople.

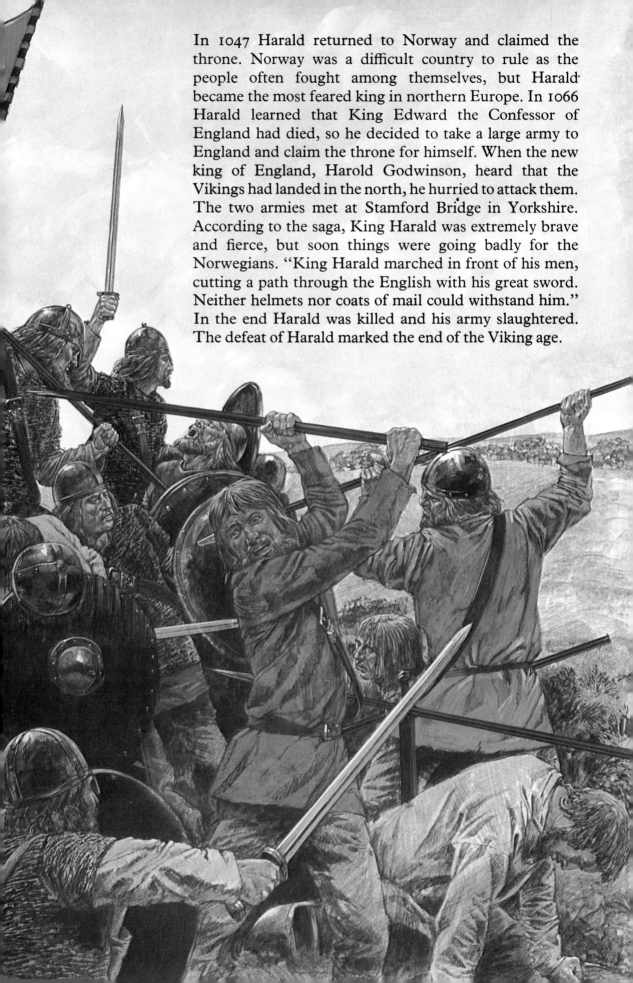

In 1047 Harald returned to Norway and claimed the throne. Norway was a difficult country to rule as the people often fought among themselves, but Harald became the most feared king in northern Europe. In 1066 Harald learned that King Edward the Confessor of England had died, so he decided to take a large army to England and claim the throne for himself. When the new king of England, Harold Godwinson, heard that the Vikings had landed in the north, he hurried to attack them. The two armies met at Stamford Bridge in Yorkshire. According to the saga, King Harald was extremely brave and fierce, but soon things were going badly for the Norwegians. "King Harald marched in front of his men, cutting a path through the English with his great sword. Neither helmets nor coats of mail could withstand him." In the end Harald was killed and his army slaughtered. The defeat of Harald marked the end of the Viking age.

The Viking sunset

The Viking raids came to an end in about 1066. However, Scandinavians continued to trade in Europe and to sail to North America to cut timber. At home, the Vikings tended to lead a more settled life, fighting far less.

Even while these raids were taking place, the kings of Norway, Sweden and Denmark were each uniting their country. This meant that people were less likely to fight each other and devoted more time to agriculture and other crafts and skills. This made the countries more prosperous and less dependent on foreign goods and skills. People were no longer so anxious to leave their homes to fight. They were happy to be farmers and craftsmen.

By the beginning of the eleventh century, the Vikings found it difficult to attack Germany, Holland, France and England. They found strong armies and fleets waiting for them, and some countries even employed Vikings to defend them. Rollo and his men, for example, guarded the northern shores of France.

During the tenth and eleventh centuries, many Vikings were converted to Christianity. The people had to abandon their own gods, which they had worshipped for hundreds of years, in favour of Christian beliefs. The coming of Christianity changed the Vikings' way of life and contributed to the lessening of their power.

▲ This is one of the oldest crucifixes yet found in Scandinavia, and dates from the tenth century. It was discovered at Birka in Sweden.

► King Harald Bluetooth of Denmark was baptized in 960. He became a Christian after seeing a missionary pick up a red-hot iron bar without burning himself.

Legacy of the Vikings

or many years people have regarded the Vikings as brutal barbarians who did nothing but loot and kill. This was not so. They did a great many constructive things as well.

The Vikings were great traders. Wherever they went they built new towns or enlarged old ones, like Kiev in Russia and Dublin in Ireland. They took furs and slaves to Constantinople and Baghdad and returned with silks, spices, precious metals and wines. They were also great explorers, and travelled as far as the Scottish Islands, Iceland, Greenland and even America. In many of these places, such as Iceland and Greenland, they founded permanent settlements.

Although the Vikings were fierce and quarrelsome, they believed in law and order. The *Althing*, an assembly which was partly a parliament and partly a law court, was the first such institution to be founded in Europe. The Viking warriors also valued their freedom. When a messenger asked to be taken to the leader of Rollo's army he was told that there was no leader, everyone was equal.

The Vikings were great artists. They decorated their weapons, furniture and houses with beautiful designs and pictures. They worked equally well in wood, iron, horn and ivory. Their boat-building skills enabled them to sail the Atlantic quite safely.

Sagas were stories, passed down by word of mouth until they were finally written down by scholars in the thirteenth century. This extract describes the Battle of Svolder in 1000, in which the brave King Olaf of Norway was defeated by King Swein of Denmark and King Olov of Sweden.

" The battle was fierce and bitter. Olaf's men threw grappling irons on to Swein's ships, but King Swein and his men escaped on to their other ships and retreated. Then King Olov came alongside and attacked, but he suffered the same fate as the others, losing many men and several ships.

But at last, all King Olaf's ships were captured except the Long Serpent. *There was such a hail of arrows and spears that Olaf's men were unable to protect themselves. King Olaf now had so few men that the enemy were able to board his ship. His crew were forced to jump overboard, where they were killed by the enemy.*

Then, King Olaf himself leapt into the water. They tried to seize him, but the king raised his shield above his head and sank forever beneath the waves."

The story of the Vikings

793

This is the accepted date of the first Viking attack on western Europe. A band of Vikings attacked and destroyed the famous monastery of Lindisfarne off the north-east coast of England. For a time the Vikings on the Continent were held in check by the great emperor Charlemagne (742-814). When he died, his empire broke up and Viking attacks began.

830

Viking fleets sailed up the rivers and over the seas into Holland, France, England and Ireland. Later they attacked Spain, but found the Moslem Moors fiercer than themselves. This did not stop them entering the Mediterranean. They even sailed to the eastern Mediterranean and looted coastal towns there.

While the Norwegians and Danes were attacking western Europe and the Mediterranean, the Swedes moved into Russia. They founded and settled in towns close to the great Russian rivers and built up a rich trade with Constantinople. Some of them crossed Russia and sailed down the River Volga to the Caspian Sea. Here,

they traded with Arab merchants fro[m] Baghdad. For some time the Varangia[n] Vikings, as they were called, repeated[ly] raided these cities. However, the Byzan[...]tines and the Arabs were too powerf[ul] for them.

▲ King Alfred flees in the face of Viking attack.

851

The Danes set up a base on the Isle [of] Sheppey in the Thames and wintered i[n] England. They were no longer content t[o] make lightning raids on Europe. The[y] were now determined to carry out con[...]centrated attacks and set up similar base[s] on islands in French and German river[s].

878

In England, Wessex was one of the las[t] Anglo-Saxon states free from Viking rule[.] The Danes, led by Guthrum, invade[d] Wessex and seized control. King Alfre[d] was forced to flee to the Isle of Athelne[y] in Somerset until he could collect hi[s] army together. Then he defeated th[e] Danes at the Battle of Edington. He mad[e] peace and allowed the Danes to continu[e] living in eastern England. This area wa[s] called the Danelaw.

▲ The Vikings attacking the Byzantines at Constantinople.

he "Great Army" crossed the Channel
England. For four years the Vikings
ied to overcome King Alfred's resis-
nce. Finally the king triumphed, and the
rmy left the country in 896.

King Charles the Fat invited Rollo and
s men to settle in Normandy to defend
s shores against other Scandinavians.
ollo agreed and was loyal and successful.

King Charles the Fat invites Rollo to settle
Normandy.

1 982, Erik the Red set sail from Iceland
d sighted a rocky and unpromising land.
e called this country "Greenland" to
tract settlers. In 986, a sailor called
jarni was blown off course and sighted
land to the west of Greenland. No one
ied to explore this new land until Leif
rikson set out. He reached Helluland
3affin Island), Markland (Labrador) and
inland (Newfoundland).

According to the saga writers, there
ere several other voyages to Vinland.
owever, Indian attacks prevented the
ikings from founding a permanent
olony in America. Expeditions continued
sail to Markland to cut timber until 1347.

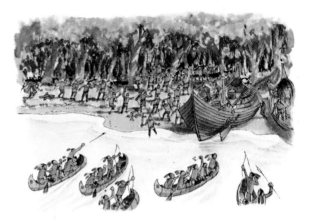

▲ The Indians forced the Vikings to
leave North America.

1002

Another great wave of Viking attacks took
place. In England, King Ethelred the
Unready (or the 'ill-advised') could not
decide how to deal with the Viking invaders.

Later, the king ordered his followers
to murder all the Vikings they could
find. It is said that Gunhild, King Swein
Forkbeard's sister, was killed in this
massacre. Certainly, Swein raided England even more often and finally con-
quered it. His son Knut, or Canute, ruled
the country between 1017 and 1035. Knut
forced the Vikings and English to live
peacefully together. In 1030, Knut defeated and killed King Olaf of Norway at
the Battle of Stiklestad and became the
master of a huge Scandinavian empire.
Unfortunately, his sons were not strong
enough to rule it after his death and the
empire collapsed.

1066

By this time the Scandinavian world was
relatively quiet and peaceful. King Harald
Hardrada attacked England but was killed
at the Battle of Stamford Bridge. The
Viking age was over.

Famous Vikings

Rollo (860-931) became the first Viking Duke of Normandy. He was originally called Rolf the Ganger or Walker. This was because his legs were so long that he could not find a horse big enough to carry him. He spent ten years attacking France before King Charles the Fat offered him land to settle on in France. In return, he defended France against all other Scandinavians. In 912, he became a Christian. William the Conqueror was one of his descendants.

Hakon I (915-960) was the first Christian king of Norway. He was educated at the court of King Athelstan of England. He returned to Norway in 935 and claimed the throne. He introduced Christianity and tried to establish law and order by setting up *things* all over Norway. He was killed in battle in 960.

Harald Bluetooth (?-986) was a king of Denmark. In the late 950s he attacked Norway. At first, King Hakon defeated him but in 960 Harald killed his rival and became king of both Denmark and Norway. Worse still, in 974, he was attacked by the armies of the German emperor, Otto II. Soon afterwards, Harald was overthrown by his ambitious son, Swein Forkbeard, and died in exile in 986.

Swein Forkbeard (986-1014) was one of the most successful kings of Denmark. He cleared the Germans out of Jutland and set about raiding his neighbours. In 994, he took part in a great attack on England. At the Battle of Svolder in 1000, he defeated and killed Olaf Tryggvason, the king of Norway. After the Massacre of St Brice's Day in 1002, Swein spent much of his time in England. He died at Gainsborough in 1014.

▲ A statue of Rollo, later Duke of Normandy

Olaf Tryggvason (968-1000) was famous king of Norway who made h name by attacking England. In 994 h attacked London with Swein Forkbear but without success. He became a Chris tian and was made King of Norway on h return. He tried hard to convert h people to Christianity, but was unsu cessful. Unfortunately, he quarrelled wit Swein Forkbeard and was killed at th Battle of Svolder in 1000.

St Olaf (?-1030) seized control of Norwa on the death of Swein Forkbeard in 101 In 1016 he was accepted as king and de voted himself to the task of converting h eople to Christianity. He was defeated in 026 at the Battle of the River Helge. In 028 Knut invaded Norway and Olaf fled o Russia. He was killed fighting bravely t the Battle of Stiklestad.

Knut the Great or Canute (1014-1035)

vas probably the greatest of the Viking kings. He continued the work of Swein Forkbeard, his father, in England and vas recognized as king in 1017. For the rest of his life he managed to persuade the Saxons and Vikings in England to live in peace. He made many wise laws. He defeated Olaf II of Norway at the Battle of Stiklestad in 1030 and became King of Norway. When he died, his empire collapsed because of the weakness of his sons.

▲ Leif Erikson, discoverer of America.

Harald Hardrada (1015-1066) was present at the Battle of Stiklestad and saw the king, his half-brother, die. He fled to Russia and made his way to the Mediterranean world. There he lived first as a pirate and then as a member of the Byzantine emperor's guard. In 1047 he returned to Norway and claimed the throne. However, it was many years before all the Norwegians accepted him. He led an expedition to England in 1066 and was killed at the Battle of Stamford Bridge by Harold Godwinson.

Erik the Red (?-1000) was brought up in south-west Norway but was outlawed for killing a man. He sailed to Iceland and made his home there. But once again, he was banished for murder. As both Iceland and Norway were closed to him, he decided to sail westwards in search of a land first sighted fifty years earlier by a sailor called Gunnbjorn. In 982, Erik came across a huge, rocky land. For the next three years, he explored its coasts. Then he returned to Iceland and collected together a large group of settlers. In 986 he led a fleet of 25 ships to what he called "Greenland". This was the start of a flourishing colony. Erik ran a successful farm at Brattahlid in south-western Greenland until his death.

Leif Erikson (?-?) was the eldest son of Erik the Red. In about 1000, he decided to go in search of a mysterious land sighted by an Icelander called Bjarni in 986. As a result, he discovered Helluland (modern Baffin Island), Markland (Labrador) and Vinland (America). On his return to Greenland he learned that his father had died. He decided to give up exploring and took over the running of the family farm at Brattahlid.

The world the Vikings knew

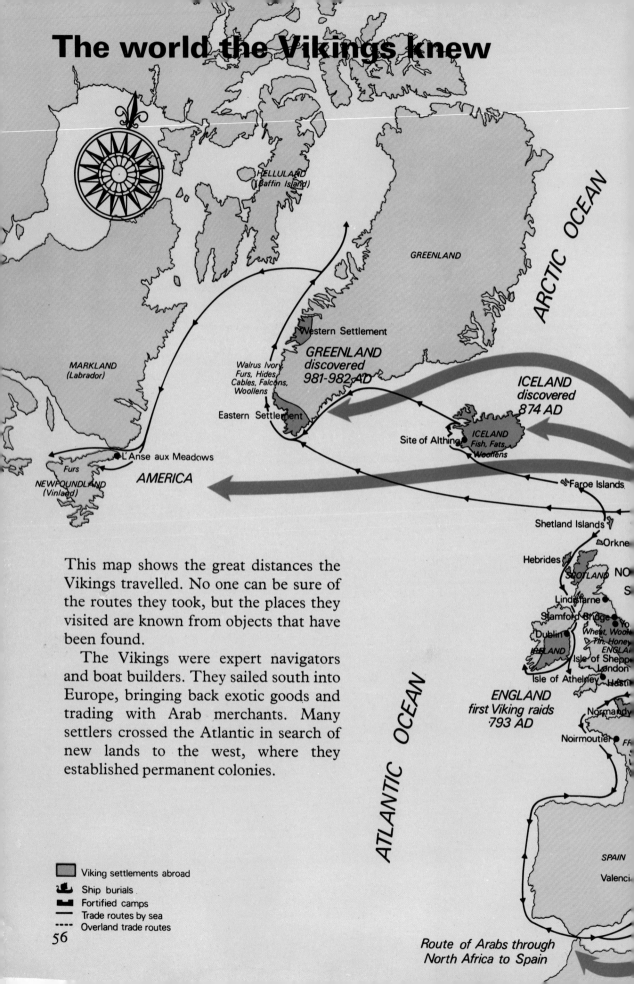

HELLULAND
(Baffin Island)

GREENLAND

ARCTIC OCEAN

Western Settlement

GREENLAND
discovered
981-982 AD

MARKLAND
(Labrador)

Walrus Ivory,
Furs, Hides,
Cables, Falcons,
Woollens

ICELAND
discovered
874 AD

Eastern Settlement

Site of Althing

ICELAND
Fish, Fats,
Woollens

L'Anse aux Meadows

Furs

Faroe Islands

NEWFOUNDLAND
(Vinland)

AMERICA

Shetland Islands

Orkne

Hebrides

SCOTLAND   NO

S

Lindisfarne

Stamford Bridge

Yo

Dublin

Wheat, Wool
Tin, Honey

ENGLA

IRELAND

Isle of Sheppe

London

Isle of Athelney

Hast

This map shows the great distances the Vikings travelled. No one can be sure of the routes they took, but the places they visited are known from objects that have been found.

The Vikings were expert navigators and boat builders. They sailed south into Europe, bringing back exotic goods and trading with Arab merchants. Many settlers crossed the Atlantic in search of new lands to the west, where they established permanent colonies.

ATLANTIC OCEAN

ENGLAND
first Viking raids
793 AD

Normandy

Noirmoutier   FR

SPAIN

Valenci

Viking settlements abroad
Ship burials
Fortified camps
Trade routes by sea
Overland trade routes

Route of Arabs through
North Africa to Spain

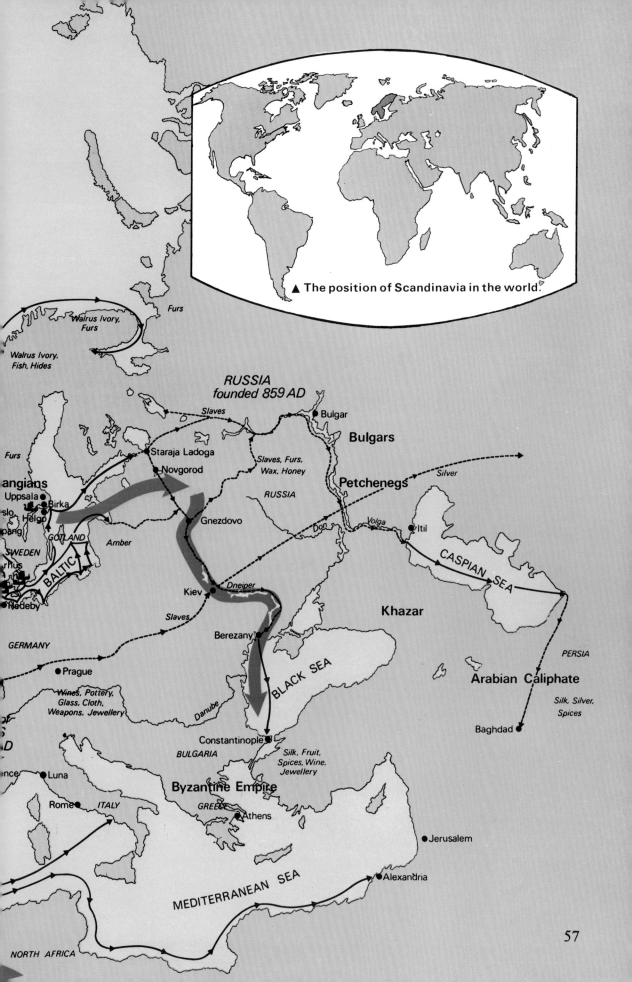

The position of Scandinavia in the world.

Walrus Ivory, Furs

Furs

Walrus Ivory, Fish, Hides

Furs

RUSSIA
founded 859 AD

Slaves

Bulgar

Bulgars

Staraja Ladoga

angians

Novgorod

Slaves, Furs, Wax, Honey

Petchenegs

Silver

Uppsala

Birka

slo

Helgö

pang

RUSSIA

Gnezdovo

Don

Volga

Itil

GOTLAND

Amber

SWEDEN

rhus

BALTIC

CASPIAN SEA

Kiev

Dneiper

Khazar

edeby

Slaves

Berezany

GERMANY

PERSIA

Prague

Arabian Caliphate

Wines, Pottery,
Glass, Cloth,
Weapons, Jewellery

Silk, Silver,
Spices

Danube

BLACK SEA

Baghdad

Constantinople

BULGARIA

Silk, Fruit,
Spices, Wine,
Jewellery

ence

Luna

Byzantine Empire

Rome

ITALY

GREECE

Athens

Jerusalem

Alexandria

MEDITERRANEAN SEA

NORTH AFRICA

57

World history AD 800 to 1100

	Vikings	Europe	Asia
AD 800	Traditionally, Lindisfarne was the first place in Europe to be attacked by the Vikings (793). After that, Germany, the Netherlands, France and the British Isles suffered almost continuous attack.	Charlemagne, king of the Franks, was crowned Holy Roman Emperor by the Pope (800). He created a large empire, including France, Germany and northern Italy. His sons quarrelled amongst themselves and divided the empire in 847. Their wars gave the Vikings the opportunity to attack Europe.	The Tang dynasty ruled Chi[na] from 611 to 907. During tha[t] time China enjoyed a "Gold[en] Age" in art. Her poetry, pain[ting] and porcelain reached particularly high standards. Japan, the Fujiwara family controlled the emperor betw[een] the mid-ninth and the twelf[th] century.
AD 860	National monarchies appeared in Norway, Denmark and Sweden. Halvdan united Norway (850) and Gorm united Denmark (860). The Swedish Vikings invaded Russia and took over the Slav cities of Novgorod and Kiev (862). During the next few years they either traded with the Byzantines or attacked them.	The Bulgars in eastern Europe were converted to Christianity (861). The Macedonian emperors ruled the Byzantine empire from 867 to 1056. Siegfried, king of the Danes, besieged Paris (885-886). Rollo became Duke of Normandy.	A great empire grew up in th[e] Mekong Valley in south-eas[t] Asia. It was ruled by the Hin[du] Khmers. Ankor was the cap[ital] of this empire. It was full of temples decorated with spl[endid] carvings.
AD 920	Harald Bluetooth of Denmark became a Christian, as did Hakon the Good of Norway. Harald invaded Norway and killed Hakon in 960.	Otto I united Germany and northern Italy. He was crowned emperor in 962. He also managed to defeat the Magyars, the wild horsemen from the Steppes, who eventually settled in Hungary.	India was divided up into a number of states. Perhaps t[he] most important people were [the] Rajputs who spread widely [in] central and northern India. Buddhism spread rapidly fr[om] India to China and Japan.
AD 980	Swein Forkbeard of Denmark defeated and killed Olaf Tryggvason of Norway at the Battle of Svolder (1000). The Massacre of St Brice's Day (1002) led to the conquest of England by Swein and Knut of Denmark. In 1028, Knut killed King Olaf and added Norway to his empire.	Basil II, the Byzantine emperor, defeated the Bulgars and destroyed their power (1014). Norman adventurers arrived in southern Italy and fought against the Byzantines. Robert Guiscard was one of their greatest leaders. They made themselves masters of southern Italy and Sicily.	The Sung dynasty (960-12[79]) came to power in China. Th[e] Sung were also famous for [their] art and inventions. They invented the abacus, printin[g] blocks, and movable type. T[hey] produced a fine encyclope[dia] and made hand-grenades o[r] gunpowder.
AD 1040	The Swedes were converted to Christianity and King Harald Hardrada of Norway made the last great Viking raid. He attacked England in 1066 and was defeated and killed at the Battle of Stamford Bridge.	El Cid, the national hero of Spain, steadily pushed back the Moslem Moors (1040-1099). Pope Gregory VII and the emperor Henry IV quarrelled over the appointment of bishops (1076). Pope Urban II preached the first crusade at Clermont (1095).	The Sung administration w[as] particularly efficient. Anyon[e] wanting to be a civil servan[t] had to pass three sets of examinations. Even then on[ly] the very best graduates we[re] chosen. Later, Europeans c[alled] these civil servants *mandar[ins]*
AD 1100			

rica	Near East	America	AD

			800
:entral Sudan was nated by the great empire nem which lasted from 800 00. It was a highly alized empire with powerful es.	A new dynasty of Caliphs called the Abbasids took over the Arab empire in 750. They made Baghdad their capital. It became a great centre of trade. Spices and minerals came from India, jewels and fabrics from central Asia, ivory and gold from Africa and silks and porcelain from China.	The Mayas, who lived in Guatemala, Yucatan and south-east Mexico, came to the end of their classical period. They built magnificent stone cities but probably did not live in them. They were only used for religious purposes.	

			AD **860**
ng the ninth century an own people built the city of abwe in Rhodesia. The consist of walled huts and osures with conical towers igantic walls.	The Arabs made great discoveries in the world of medicine. For example, Al Razi (860-935) discovered many ways of treating measles and smallpox. He wrote 200 text books before he died. In mathematics, the Arabs brought the numerals 1-9 from India and introduced 0 themselves.	The Maya civilization suffered a widespread decline, coming to an end in parts of Mexico and Guatemala. However, they continued to flourish in Yucatan. The Toltecs conquered the Valley of Mexico and made Tula their capital.	

			AD **920**
mpire of Ghana was set up st Africa. It was famous for and slaves and sold both to eoples living in north a. The Ghanaians were ems and their cities ained beautiful mosques.	The Abbasid empire broke up into a number of smaller empires. For example, the Fatimids seized control of north Africa.	The Toltecs invaded the Maya empire. Although they absorbed many Maya ideas, they were basically a race of warriors. As a result, there was a period of almost continuous war. In South America, Peru was dominated first by Tiahuanaco and then by the Chimu in the north.	

			AD **980**
Africa was dominated by atimids from 908 onwards. gradually made their way nd conquered Egypt in 969 , they took over Palestine, and Arabia. In the eleventh ry the Almoravids took place in north Africa.	The Seljuk Turks forced their way into the Near East from the Russian Steppes. In 1038, they invaded Persia and seized Baghdad (1058). The Seljuks swept all before them and decided to attack the Byzantine empire.	The warlike Toltecs conquered many smaller, independent states, and became rulers of most of west Mexico. Chichen Itza became a Toltec city.	

			AD **1040**
lmoravids conquered west a and converted many of the le to the Moslem religion. rds 1100 the Yoruba empire created near the mouth of ver Niger. The people ed a high level of ation and made exquisite es.	In 1071, the Seljuks defeated the Byzantines and the emperor was forced to ask the Pope and the rulers of western Europe for help. The crusaders conquered the Holy Land but refused to hand it over to the Byzantines. Instead, they set up states of their own.	The Miztec tribe expanded under the leadership of their chief, Eight-Deer Ocelot Claw. In Peru, the Chimu people created a coastal empire, stretching for six hundred miles. The city of Tula was destroyed by invading northern tribes.	AD **1100**

Glossary

althing the National Assembly and law courts of Iceland.

archaeologist expert who studies the past from its physical remains.

Asgard the kingdom of the Viking gods.

blood feud dangerous quarrel that lasted for several generations.

bridesprice money or goods a husband-to-be had to give his future bride's father.

buttermilk milk left after churning.

charcoal charred, blackened wood.

clinker-built ship made of overlapping planks.

dowry gifts given by a father to his daughter on her marriage.

fiord long arm of the sea running deep into the land.

futhark runic alphabet.

hand-quern small hand mill for grinding corn.

Heimskringla collection of sagas written by Snorri Sturluson.

jarl free farmer.

karl rich freeman.

long house rectangular house.

longship canoe-like warship.

loom frame on which yarn is woven into cloth.

mail armour made of small metal rings.

petty king a king who ruled a small part of a larger country.

runes Viking alphabet.

saga heroic story or history passed down by word of mouth.

scythe tool for cutting grass or corn.

serf peasant who worked the land for rich farmers.

spoor tracks made by animals.

thing an assembly where local issues were discussed and criminals were brought to justice.

thrall slave.

Valhalla the heaven where Viking warriors went after death.

Valkyries spirit maidens who led dead warriors to Valhalla.

Vinland Viking name for America.

wattle and daub building fabric made of sticks covered with clay.

yarn thread used in the making of cloth.

Index